Figured Dark

Figured Dark

**Poems by
Greg Rappleye**

The University of Arkansas Press

Fayetteville ■ 2007

Copyright © 2007 by The University of Arkansas Press

11   10   09   08   07   5   4   3   2   1

Text design by Ellen Beeler

⊛ The paper used in this publication meets the minimum requirements
of the American National Standard for Permanence of Paper for Printed
Library Materials Z39.48-1984.

Library of Congress Cataloging-in-Publication Data

Rappleye, Greg.
Figured dark : poems / by Greg Rappleye.
    p. cm.
  ISBN-13: 978-1-55728-852-3 (pbk. : alk. paper)
  ISBN-10: 1-55728-852-6 (pbk. : alk. paper)
  Title.
  PS3568.A6294F54 2007
  811'.6—dc22
                                                    2007024796

For Marcia, Always

Only dispossessed people know their land in the dark.

—*Elizabeth Bowen*

Acknowledgments

My thanks to the editors of the journals in which these poems
first appeared, sometimes in slightly different forms:
"Letter to M., from Swannanoa" and "Lilacs, for Instance,"
Bellingham Review; "At 48, Walking My Baby Past the Voodoo
Lounge," "The Fish Lamp on the Cover of *Coastal Living*
Magazine," and "Obbligato," *Blue Mesa Review;* "Mason's
Kitchenettes," *Clark Street Review;* "At the Museum of Whiskey
History," "Descent," and "Hay Devil," *Driftwood Review;*
"Biopsy," *Georgetown Review;* "Not that Happiness," *Greensboro
Review;* "In the Great Field at Mount Holyoke, under a Dome
of Stars," *Legal Studies Forum;* "On a Visit to His Namesake
City, St. Paul Walks Six Blocks of Goodrich Avenue," *Louisiana
Literature;* "Caller, What is Your Question?," "My Mother
Thinks She's Peggy Lee," "Near Gatlinburg," and "Rainy
Afternoon at the Gotham Book Mart," *Margie: The American
Journal of Poetry;* "Lost-Love Ghazals," *Marlboro Review;*
"Making a Path to the Blackberries" and "After the Divorce"
(under the title "Shunned"), *Poem;* "Blackbirds," *Poetry;* "Self-
portrait, with Epiphany to Come," *Prairie Schooner;* "Gentians,"
Rhino; "Archie Babcock Explains the Accident to John
Berryman's Biographer," *River City;* "Exile Valise" and "In
Ambient Light," *River Styx;* "After an Illustration by Rockwell
Kent for *Moby-Dick,* in Which a Whale Takes a Dory in its Maw,
and Heads for the Bottom of the Sea," *Runes;* "Letter to the
Chairwoman of the Reunion Committee," *Southeast Review;*
"Elegy for Light and Balance," *Southern California Anthology;*
"Discontinuous Narrative," "For the Lord G-d Bird, No Longer
Extinct," and "Were We Speaking, Had You Asked," *Southern
Poetry Review;* "Glaucoma," *Southern Review;* "Memories of
Pittsburgh and Stern," *Spillway;* "Carolina Woodpecker," *Tar
River Poetry;* "The Salt Cairn," *Virginia Quarterly Review;*
"Black Dog," *West Branch.*

"Archie Babcock Explains the Accident to John Berryman's
Biographer," "Caller, What is Your Question?," "Letter to the
Chairwoman of the Reunion Committee," "Lilacs, for

Instance," "Making a Path to the Blackberries," "Rainy Afternoon at the Gotham Book Mart," and "After the Divorce" (under the title "Shunned") were reprinted in the *Legal Studies Forum*.

"In Ambient Light" also appeared in "Verse Daily."

"In the Great Field at Mount Holyoke, under a Dome of Stars" also appeared in *Joyful Noise: An Anthology of American Spiritual Poetry* (Autumn House Press, 2007).

"Blackbirds" also appeared in the "Poem a Day" series of the Poetry Foundation, on the Martha Stewart Living Radio Network (Sirius Satellite Network).

My gratitude to Priscilla Atkins, Jane Bach, and Jack Ridl for helpful comments on these poems. Special thanks to Lisa Olson, to the Warren Wilson community of writers, and to Toi Derricotte, Michael Collier, and the good people at the Bread Loaf Writers' Conference. My eternal gratitude to Enid Shomer.

Contents

I

II

III

Figured Dark

I

In the Great Field at Mount Holyoke, under a Dome of Stars

I said, Lord, let me speak.
I am wearied by their honeysuckle words,
their kamikaze advice.

To the south are the lights of Springfield.
North stands the house of Emily,
your difficult servant.

Save me as I travel north.

Let me stand watch
under dead Tom's plum-colored sky
and disappear again as I vanished tonight,
into Eamon's gather dark.

And the Lord said, *Keep silent.*

And the Lord said, *Dance as a child dances,*
so I dizzied myself in the field.

And the Lord said, *On this star-hammered night*
slap neither the mosquito nor the gnat,
for it is me, come at last
to whisper in your ear.

Caller, What is your Question?

The Diane Rehm Show

I'm driving. Diane's with an expert
on the birds of Costa Rica.
She goes to Nick in Bayonne
who drones on about his parakeet,
dead these forty-odd years.
I imagine her staring at the second hand—
the long weary sweep of it.
Poor Nick! But what about Diane,
out there on the baby-bird legs of her voice?
She can hardly *talk*—has *spasmodic dysphonia,*
and every six weeks goes off the air
to have Botox injected directly
into her larynx—one hundred ccs of death, straight,
no chaser—what about *her* pain,
Mr. Whosis from Bayonne?
So I punch the accelerator
and switch to the passing lane,
then push the button for the AM side,
where every voice is my father's voice
and no one *cares* about your question,
moron—the ball is dead, the rims are dead,
the salary cap is killing the game, no way
Tiger can handle the quick greens,
the slick new fairways—oh, I am
too stupid to live! Locked-and-loaded,
I flip back, loathing the trumpet
that volleys against the piano
in Diane's theme and hating the man
still buzzing like a gnat

around his insipid, self-referential little point,
until I'm shouting, What do you *want,*
you needy, dim-witted bastard—
what is your *question?* And yes,
Diane, yes, I'll hang up and take my answer
off the air.

Rainy Afternoon at the Gotham Book Mart

The sign reads *Wise Men Fish Here*
and away from the slanting rain
is a miraculous draught of books:
old novels, first editions, an entire wall
of poetry. The center table spills over,
as if a trawler has just dropped
a thousand titles onto a raised deck.
I find Allen Tate's *Collected,*
an anthology of Czech poets
in face-on-face translations
and a print of the famous photograph,
"A Collection of Poets"—the reception
in 1948 for Edith and Osbert Sitwell.
They are posed center-left
at the rear of this narrow room,
for what Elizabeth Bishop called "a party
in a subway train," circled by Stephen Spender,
Marianne Moore, Tennessee Williams,
the famous and the now-neglected others.
To the right, that's Bishop and Randall Jarrell,
in the foreground, Delmore Schwartz,
all in the shadow of Auden, who has draped himself,
Christ-like, across a black stepladder.
I've seen the article from *Life*,
with its gushy Sitwell headlines:
"They Sprang From a Famous Family,"
"They Brave New York," six pages
spread among the adverts for Minit Rub
and Studebaker, for Lucky Strikes
and Apple Pyequick. This print

is one exposure *after* the one in *Life*.
See for yourself—this head turned,
a poet's arm raised. Jarrell and Bishop,
who've been discussing Rilke, now look
stage-left and out of the frame, as if
already seeking an exit. Schwartz,
who interrupted them to press
some obscurity with Jarrell,
has gone slack jawed,
as if he's just foreseen the years to come.
I go back to the shelves, where I find
Delmore Schwartz: Life of an American Poet,
With its 1961 photo: Schwartz, seated
in Washington Square—
destitute, averting his eyes,
his cigarette held in the familiar style,
a tabloid, headline screaming
HEIRESS KEEPS HER MILLIONS,
tossed beneath the bench.
I pay for the books, the famous print,
and for an extra dollar, buy a plastic sleeve
to keep it safe, then step through the jangle-bell door
into the rain on West Forty-seventh—*The rain
that slants from the crowded light, The rain
of pour and pouring down,*—a storm
that Bishop told us *Will roar all night.*

Not that Happiness

Not bluebirds nesting in a wooden box
nailed to your picket fence.
No geraniums in the planter, but yarrow
where the trees begin, hawkweed
in a clearing near the black locust
and loosestrife—how you are helpless
against its beauty—everywhere
along the creek. No friends anymore
who ask about dinner, but a boy who woke
last week, singing counterpoint
to the wrens. To read, *We are without*
consolation or excuse, and remember
a sack of peaches from the roadside stand;
hunger the day you stopped for them.
Maxine Sullivan singing "Blue Skies."
In winter, lullabies sung for the dead.
The shoulder roast simmering in red wine
with potatoes and sweet onions
on a day when the rain begins; your heart
sliding toward the sinkhole of November.
Who is not captive to some small happiness?
To love a field you can never own—the pink mist
of knapweed, the blue of chicory.
Or the heron that settles in the neighbor's pond
and croaks through the last of your dreams.
You startle awake, patting your head, glad
that you are not a minnow, darting
among the muddy reeds. How it comes around,
this happiness, like a landlord sniffing out the rent.
Not what you ordered—penny whistles, cellophane hats,

those hand-crank noisemakers—but the happiness
that finds you, scrawls a receipt, says,
"You paid for this," whatever happiness is.

Black Dog

There's a black dog under my house.
Hear him growl and moan.
He sends the cat up the traveler's palm
and keeps the postman from my door.

There are days I call him out,
rolling baseballs through the yard.
He gnaws through the stitches,
unravels the strings. He wants
the bounce of the hard rubber core.

Then come nights when the moon is full
and the black dog howls it down.
Tourists cross themselves
as the moon sinks on a reef of stars.
O, the charry planets of his eyes!

I feed him sweetmeats,
chuck steaks, *carbonados* of veal—
nothing but the best for *my* dog!
He gnaws and farts and burns the lawn
with his sulphurous amber pee.

And black dog will not leave.

A fortune I've spent on this dog.
He's cost me everything.
Ship wracker, salvor—snapping
his own fur and mouthfuls of air—
this growler stares me down.
I nail his photograph,
this blood mark at my door.

Self-portrait, with Epiphany to Come

How the portrait changes, depending
on where you stand. The background split
between indigo sky and yellow clapboard,
the subject in blues and flesh tones,
jean jacket over his frayed shirt,
tired around his hazel eyes
but looking straight at the painter—
a torso in its middle years.
Thus has the Lord dealt with me, in the days
wherein he looked on me.
Blues for grief, earth tones because
he's made of earth,
burnt sienna and cadmium green,
as if the man is wholly finished
disavowing the odds. Note the painter's
obsession, how he goes back to his blues,
lost in the sad octaves.
And just there—an ill-lit cloud,
the slight turbulence in a brush stroke—
you'll find an angel, fluttering to wake.
Not that the painter wanted this—
how could he? Not a canvas set to erupt,
not that damn shiny creature
come again to speak.

For the Lord G-d Bird, No Longer Extinct

[The] announcement brought rejoicing among birdwatchers, for whom the ivory bill has long been a holy grail—a creature that has been called the Lord God bird, apparently because that is what people exclaimed when they saw it.

—*The New York Times*

A lost god, it knows a hundred
lost names: King Logcock, Lord Chuckaluck,
Whackadoodle, What-the-fuck.
A creature so marvelous that Audubon,
who—*Blam!*—shot a baker's dozen,
called it the work of a master:
"The glossy body and tail, the white
slashes on its wings and neck,
that ivory bill, lit by the vermilion
of the male's pendent crest;
the stalking yellow of its eye.
When I see one swoop from tree to tree,
I shout, 'There goes a Rembrandt!'"
Some name the bird for its call,
however they may hear it—
Kint-kint, kent-kent, can't-can't.
Some for its look; that heavenly mix
of schizophrenia and doom—
Crimson-headed Noodlebird, Blood-
on-the-Ax, Cassie-Get-the-Scattergun,
Old Scramble Brains. A god-like bird
and a God so mysterious, so
blue-smoke-and-mirrors-gone-from-this-world,
the holy ones won't write His full name,
always dropping a vowel,

like orphans trailing bread crumbs
through a fairy tale woods: Ad-nai,
El-him, Jeh-vah Shammah,
Jeh-vah Shalom. What's gone
is the "O" of surprise—a poet's trick,
but O, the thrill of finding alive
what was long thought dead!
The ornithologist, after four shaky seconds
of videotape, in which the extinct
went—*can't-can't!*—flapping across a creek, collapsed
in the ranger's arms and wept, "I saw an ivory bill!"
As if God himself might finally be found
alive in the Malookas—
the Ancient of Days, banging
against a tree, drilling the heartwood,
still obsessed with digging out
whatever worms within.

At the Museum of Whiskey History

I find my dead, sneaking shots of Old Crow
on the line at Kelsey-Hayes—
bootleggers, priests, procession swellers.
Here's Uncle Ted saying, *Cheers to you all,*
after beating a black man senseless
behind a blind pig. And there's Aunt Rose,
fresh from the San, taking it neat,
after hacking a fistful of blood. My dead
drive from the freight yards and Dodge Main,
drunk for the Teamsters and drunk
for Walter Reuther, shattering windows
and tipping over cars.
They marry among the hill folk, who come
rattle-trapping north to work at Ford Rouge.
See their anemic wives—
my aunts with their melon-headed kids.
There's my mother, retching among the violets
and my father's foot tap-tapping the rail
after Sunday mass, needing
two shots of Jim Beam before a game of skittles,
the stone sent gliding along the boards,
sawdust parting in its wake.
And in this diorama,
where the warehouse burns
and the whiskey flows in rivers of fire
torching the sumac and yarrow, my dead
toast the flames. My dead fall down.
My dead rise from the ground and sing.

My Mother Thinks She's Peggy Lee

The svelte chanteuse dyes her hair
champagne blond, wraps herself
in a spangly robe, and settles
with an Asti and orange juice
to watch Arthur Godfrey. I set up
a TV tray and my three-string
ukulele. I'm the co-host!
She sure can sing "Manana."
I thank her, salute the boys in the band—
my fingers thrown straight at the saxophones.
I introduce the scabby little cat
and our next guest—my baby sister!
after SpaghettiOs, it's Art Linkletter.
Peggy stirs a whiskey and Coke,
lies back to share a musical insight—
how Johnnie Ray, hitting the high note in "Cry,"
always thrilled her. Now, Peggy
arcs it down, sings, "Softly, As I Leave You,"
something smoky caught in her throat.
The audience is knocked out!
By four, she's asleep on the couch.
Did you catch our variety show?
We were boffo! This was
years before "Is That All There Is?"
Years before she fell from the stage
in Vegas, blowing a disc.
Before the valve job on her bum heart
and the "virus pneumonia."
Before the hard years, when that poised
ingratiating ingénue packed her bags
and disappeared.

Gentians

Naked, I hold my finger to my lips,
eyes wide, the field green and rising
behind me. No horizon, though the air
is honey-lit, wine-lit. Somewhere,
a hive, busy with the tremulous work of bees.
Amid the matted hair of my chest
and the root of my sex,
purple flowers with sea-green leaves
begin to bud, massing where the hair is massed.
And from these, gentians spread across the field,
as the bees work in a peaceful drone
while I keep my finger to my lips,
having dreamed this through those long years
I had nothing to say.

Near Gatlinburg

God is alive, programming all night radio
for Knoxville, Tennessee.
How else to explain why "Love is Alive,"
Gary Wright's great aching chestnut,
comes on as my car inches
toward the burnt out Kenworth on I-40?

Because I won't go on tonight
beyond the next exit,
I'll hear the story at breakfast—
how wheel bearings overheated,
until the cab began to sputter and melt.
When the driver was finally flagged down,
the trailer was in flames
and seventy-eight hogs in back
were scorched and squealing.

The driver did what had to be done—
he unlocked the gate, and those pigs
that didn't break their legs
broke lose in the westbound lane, and so
I'm working a slalom of flares
and wounded hogs, shattered cars with air bags
popped, the elaborate red-amber whirl
of strobe lights.

My soul is a wheel that's turning.
I love the start-and-stop of this song,
the second thoughts and double takes,
the bass line that carries me
into the next lane,

where a cop waggles his flashlight,
meaning, *Come along now, slowly.*

Some of the hogs were disemboweled.
Some had the shit knocked out
in a literal sense. Others are lost,
defecating in the dark.
But because God works his play list
or is busy, banging out another solar system
along the edge of the galaxy,
He won't stop the carnage.
The truth is, God lives in the City of Angels
and sent this song beyond the skirl
of the ionosphere,
then back to a satellite dish
in Knoxville, Tennessee.
God knows I need a soundtrack,
knows *My heart is on fire,* that
a great hog staggers along the edge of my high beams,
froth at his mouth and a clot
oozing at his shoulder.

Two deputies approach the bloody pig,
three shots ring out
and the pig drops and steams
as I crawl past.
The only way out now is to drive out,
meaning one final lane change
before I am waved back to speed.
The songs blinks away on two repeating notes,
I am within the black-and-white lines,
Alive, alive, alive.

After the Divorce

If it must be winter,
let it be absolutely winter.
                    —Linda Gregg

I think of a burned car in a field
and how the goats graze on
as the body rusts away.
At market you cross the aisle
to finger the leeks, pretend to weigh
a melon in your hands.
At first, the quiet is grievous,
which is to say, wounded
by a memory of loss,
then it is not so hard.
Months go by and it is enough—
the hours alone in the afternoon,
reading, slicing a pear.
It is August, then it is not.
Silence builds in the cicadas' absence.
Gold or a blood red burdens the leaves
until they fall, opening a vastness
in the wood lot. Winter soon.
A winter that is more and more
my home.

After an Illustration by Rockwell Kent For *Moby-Dick*, in which a Whale Takes a Dory in its Maw, and Heads for the Bottom of the Sea

Through a night-sea, through krill,
chased down by stars.
The albacores scurry away.
An ocean, otherwise, so calm.
The spears are gone, the whale's awl,
a bucket with which we might have bailed.

It was the middle of a marriage,
eight years before the break.
From Provincetown, we rode to the whales
aboard a watching boat,
and from their pod, one rose along the rail—
barnacled, his breath so foul
I did not want to be consumed.
As if the legend might be true—
we could be swallowed alive, descend
to the sea grass and marl
and live to tell of it.

Last week, this dream: waves
like an endless field, a battered dory,
the furious oars.
As the watching-boat turned,
I saw the whale rise—blue skin
breaking the surface, a vast swirl
of tail and the closure around it.
When I said *Look!* the whale was gone.
. There was only the clatter of that engine
and the wake, gun-metaled, churning upon itself.

Lost-Love Ghazals

November, when I do not love you anymore.
Snow on the last apples, I do not love you anymore.

Consigned to the river I will explain myself.
No illusions that I love you anymore.

Not the steelhead come to spawn. Not the crows.
Nothing that swims or flies loves you anymore.

The current says your name around my knees.
No matter; I do not love you anymore.

I wept for you until a century ended.
I gave up whiskey and cannot love you anymore.

Steelhead drifting below the cedar trees—
little ghost, I do not love you anymore.

You keep a bird's-eye view.
Is this a man who loves you anymore?

In the wood lot, dark unspools from the dark.
I kiss the day goodbye, not loving you anymore.

Chicken and red wine, an easy salad.
I stare out at the trees, not loving you anymore.

I built a fire and read French novels.
Bovary c'est moi. I do not love you anymore.

The silk robe falling open at your waist!
I will go to Paris and not love you anymore.

Fire became ash, a flat stone sank in the river.
I drank with the fish and did not love you anymore.

Forget me darling, forget me not.
Remind me not to love you anymore.

I wake at 3 AM and turn the lock.
Could it be you do not love me anymore?

It may have been the song of a dying man.
The dead are gone and do not love you anymore.

Why bury my name in some final couplet?
Bereft of name, I will not love you anymore.

Feeder

I bolt the grinder to my worktable
and slowly feed the blades
pink-marbled fat and bits of meat
cut from the bellies
of Herefords and Black Angus.
I mix in the confettied shreds of my poems
and pat this into a great lumpy mass
I wedge into a butcher's net
and hang from the lowest branch
of the hemlock tree. There,
the cardinals, the jays, the cowbirds,
the shiny starlings, and the finches, peck
and gnaw and worry and preen.
The birds fly over the stark red cane
of the blueberry field and into a thicket
of witchhazel, then flit along the creek
that trickles at the edge of the woodlot.
They loop back along the fence
and splatter the glass of a pickup truck
driven by a man leaning forward
to tune a staticky radio, as dusk gathers
and the birds, always hungry, fly home.

Archie Babcock Explains the Accident to John Berryman's Biographer

"Trouble," Berryman *had written in his poem, "Travelling South,"*
"but trouble that would soon be past."
　　　　—Paul Mariani, Dreamsong: The Life of John Berryman

He should have never gone to sleep
so near the road.
My brother Gordon thought dead animal,
or a package fallen off the REA truck
that ran from Detroit to Mackinaw.
This was 1939, years before the bridge.
He steers close and something pops
a lamp. *Whap!* Still don't know
what it was, so we go back to look.
A bloody mess and that boy,
blowing bubbles out his nose.
Put a dent the size of a melon
in Gordon's '35 Ford.
You should've seen that kid—
name was Bob Berryman?—
spitting porcelain, like he'd eaten
Aunt Ad's tea cups.
I remember thinking,
That fella's gonna want a new mouth.
We tossed him in the rumble seat
and scooted back up north.

■ ■

He moaned through Topinabee,
his face like a chewed plum, all
twenty-three miles to the State Police.

The desk sergeant said,
What am I s'posed to do with him?
Haul his ass to General."
Gordon'n me lugged him between us,
the kid's head waggling 'round,
blood purpling the linoleum floor.
"Lord have mercy!" the orderly said,
when that boy fell into bed.
A trooper'd tailed us from the post
so we told him what we knew.
You say that kid was somebody?
He *looked* like nobody.
This was the Depression—
bums along the road were common as skunks.
Sure, we'd been drinking,
but we'd driven that boy all the way to Cheboygan.
The cop took our names and let us go.

■ ■

Three days later, that kid's brother,
your John Berryman, is drunk at the Pinehurst.
Who amongst you knows the Babcocks?
Well, *ever-body* knows the Babcocks,
though it was the waitress,
Elsie Hollipeter, let slip we lived near Wolverine.
Aunt Ad says, "You boys better hightail it."
So we grabbed two sleeping bags
and head for Wildwood. Hell,
I could go there now and no city boy
could find me. Brush thick as a lawyer's file
and trails the Chippewas don't know!
The next day, John Berryman shows
at Uncle Les and Aunt Ad's.
He's wearing a business suit, wire glasses,
carrying a book of poems, talking

Troy and Agamemnon.
Aunt Ad thought it so strange,
she made him write it down.
Well, she ain't heard from Archie,
"Pro'lly fishing; could be gone for weeks.
Too bad about your brother's teeth,
but Lester don't know nothing
and Russell's only three."
Berryman posed by the mantle,
finger marking a place in his book,
then sat at the kitchen table,
mumbling *Agamemnon.*
Then he walked to the iron bridge
and stared for the longest time
into the Sturgeon River.

■ ■

The war came and I saw worse
on Tarawa and Saipan.
You say that poem's famous?
Read it for me again.
And let that young man rise. In the flowing dark
The pines consumed the moon and the moon of blood.
Well, he's right about the moon.
Gordon'n me were in Wildwood,
camped on Nine Mile Hill,
where you can see the valley
and trouble along the road.
Gordon stood at the fire,
the moon, blood-red the way it says,
simmering along his shoulder.
Must've been that same moon.
Gordon? Dead these thirty-eight years.
Caught a Mauser through the heart
at Bastogne.

That Berryman kid—he was passing through.
Shouldn't have slept on the goddamn road,
but we were country people
and no one meant him any harm.

Exile Valise

I'm packing my exile valise,
cut from an indigo rug
and starred with appliqués,
stitched with gold and silver thread.
In it, my yellow sweater,
still redolent of salmon roe,
the Bakelite radio I played as a child,
a mirror in which I've watched myself
age. I'm taking a sketchbook,
two fly rods, a Scout knife
for mumblety-peg, a disc of Sonny Rollins
playing "How are Things in Glocca Morra?,"
blue bottles to hang in the trees.
I have a cane for my gout-foot,
goat-foot, (bad-foot that twitches
when acid swells along the nerve),
a broken compass, unsure of true north.
I've pushed a carnation
through my ragged lapel, include
cut glass from an old chandelier,
because I admire its work with sunlight—
how light becomes one thing,
then another,—a few milky opals
to trade along the way.
If they say, *How pitiful he looks!*
If they say, *Oh, how a mighty has fallen!*
Fear not. I go with Tobit's sweet dog
and the Angel Raphael,
have Sibley's *Book of Birds* and a field guide
to the stars, with which I find the Swan,
great wings flapping in the northern sky.

I hoist my valise across my back
and dance a staggered samba,
sing *Shang a-lang a-lang*
in my Midwestern tongue—call it
tinkered brass—it is at least
a voice that I have. I'm coming to live
in a house near the inland sea,
turn on your porch light, bang
your spoon against your copper pans
to guide me home, I'm dancing
this way and that so my ears catch the sound,
I look back and the sweet dog moans,
but my angel, running ahead,
calls, *Come on, come on.*

II

Sail On, Sailor

The lonely sea looks good.
        —Brian Wilson

The ancient gods played tricks,
pulling on bird skins to flutter among us—
here, the magpies all a-clatter, there,
a horny swan. The truth is, we liked it—
lolling among the sulphurous vapors,
puzzling out the meaning of a line.
Until *do-nothingness* bored them
and a god would crank down on a crescent moon
to say *Get up and get going!* Consider
Odysseus—years after slaying the suitors—
pie-eyed, fat, and drunk.
Athena works a simple spell
and *the lonely sea looks good again,*
though by now, Homer had doddered away.
Lacking consistent authors, these last tales
are fragments, the shards nesting
in smaller and smaller baskets—
a series of alternate end-notes
in the *Mythology* of Graves.
Does Odysseus step on a stingray
while searching for conch shells, and die
when the venom eensie-weensies up his leg?
Or does Dante get it right? Odysseus,
sailing west, augers the Big Kahuna of all waves
within landfall of Purgatory,
that sung-of Kokomo. No matter.
The taste for Odysseus fades
among the Greeks, caught in a wave

of civic pride and gathering capital—
his story one more toga flick
on *Dialing for Drachmas,*
the dub out of synch with the actors' lips.
Years go by, centuries pinwheel
across the screen, until the story's told again
in *Brook Watson and the Shark*—
water streaming through his bushy, bushy blond hair
and the men straining at the oars,
a painting so perfectly posed—the fetch of the waves
and the toothy shark chomping against them,
the naked boy so near the shark's mouth,
we must finally look at the living man and say
Oh, it only ate your leg! Which is the *point* of the story,
though the lonely sea's not looking so good now,
is it? Looping us to Brian Wilson,
making sweet harmony in *Deuce Coupe*
and *Pet Sounds,* until the Sixties end
and Mr. Id begins to unravel.
Brian's in Malibu, cutting a demo with Van Dyke Parks,
the demigod of lyrics. Brian's feet
are in a sandbox—he loves the beach
but fears the smog-brown sea,
the baggies-drooping sea—
and he sits at a keyboard, torching a joint,
the spring-tide of serotonin
receding in his brain, begging
Hypnotize me so I don't go crazy.
But Van Dyke yells, *Shut up and play the song!*
Oh, su-weet song,
leftover from the aborted *Smile,*
lost grail of the Beach Boys. Brian sighs
the tape rolls, he plinks the chords
for an ancient chant
set to a galleyed beat,

like a conch lifted to the same ear,
three millennia after it was pulled from the surf:
I sailed an ocean, unsettled ocean . . .

Making a Path to the Blackberries

Wild, deeper that I've been,
variously lensed as the eyes of a wasp,
bodies that will purple my lips,
stinging them with sweetness.
Each day I hack at the thicket
while the thorns of a thousand brambles
stipple and rip my skin.
At dusk I stare at what I've done,
beeswax and menthol
rubbed in against the blistering.
I'm making a new path—
tired of the scumble of weeds,
sick of nightshade and understory.
I hear the crows clatter and preen,
already claiming their range.
Ragged wings, ragged wings,
the world is easy for them, I think.
They are magicians palming a dark coin.
Better I should build a fence, plant an orchard,
perhaps a northern peach.
Or make—What?—a pointless beauty—
the roses I promised
that would climb the new fence
like a small lyric.
But I say *Blackberries.*
The crows are feasting in the trees.
And the machete loves its work,
the dead pitched at the living green.

Figured Dark

I'm walking the iron bridge,
ascending through pitch pines and loblollies,
my right arm counting the beat
in a half-forgotten poem,
a man marking time on a summer night.
My stars are the many stars.
My song is "Moon and Sand," the moment
Chet Baker finally pulls the trumpet from his lips
and begs, in that sweet morphined drone,
"Oh, when shall we meet again?"
I think of Whistler's *Nocturne in Black and Gold*—
the shiny black of it,
the cobalt green and indigo blue,
the fireworks pop-popping over the river
and sputtering down across Cremorne Gardens.
The silvery white must be a bit of skyline
caught in the rockets' flash.

I come to the great field, fireflies
rising from the black grass. I say to no one:
The sway of her breasts as she crossed the room,
as if to decipher a small archeology—
glass beads, a needle carved out of bone.
I know that Whistler sold his easel
to cover his debts.
And Chet Baker—I saw the film—
did he jump or was he thrown
from that open window?
Even he was puzzled as he fell.
I am alone in the great field,
accounting for loss under the many,

many stars. I am amazed by fireflies.
I could round this down to a million tiny bodies,
blazing the midnight trees.

Memories of Pittsburgh and Stern

You haven't suffered, he says.
Not like we suffered in Pittsburgh.
A ratty coat and the wind whipping
down French Street.
Or twelve straight at Bessemer,
sparks fizzy around your waist
every time they poured.
Take Jack Gilbert,
smashing scorpions with a frying pan.
Or Phil Levine. Phil's from Detroit,
but he knew how to suffer.
This was years before air conditioning.
Phil, Jack, and Gerry, slaving poems
all summer in Pittsburgh.
Read Hikmet, he says, Hikmet *died*
for poetry. You? Never even had to eat
Heinz tomato soup.
He says Hikmet was really a baker
in a little place on Third.
The heat in that bakery!
Kneading dough, singing out poems!
Monongahela! That's five syllables—he'd sing,
Allegheny! That's four. The air so thick
with yeast, he'd sing those river names
so you knew he was there.

American Kestrel

Though you were watching me,
I neither ate nor drank, but what
you saw was a vision.
                              —Tobit 12:19

Atop the pole, a kestrel.
The field? Not yet green,
though it was a day between storms
and the sun was doing its work.
I was resting in the light-filled air
and the cottonwoods along the river
were letting go their cottony seeds—
wind blowing, trees letting go.
The seeds were like angels, ascending
and descending in the breeze.
It was male, this kestrel,
with a steely crown and rufous breast
and false eyes at the nape of his neck.
His talons were maize, the yellow
of summer corn. I know this
because I have a book of raptors,
a book that was written
for use in the field,
and every illustration, every word
is directed to that end.
The kestrel sang a kestrel's song.
Killy, killy are the words.
And the kestrel rose from the pole
kiting in the wind
to sing and search the field.
Though he was small as raptors go,

he seemed a great angel
wheeling among cherubim, searching
with his true eyes.
I did not so much see as dream this—
how the kestrel wheeled
in the blue air,
then struck the field in a flurry of wings.
Yes, the kestrel killed the mouse.
I knew before I saw the bird
lift the body and tear the flesh.
*The little king at work in the field, lifting
the body and tearing the flesh.*
The body seemed a great weight.
The blood stained the kestrel's talons
and his rufous red breast. The blood
made true his *killy, killy* song.
But the angels went on, rising
and falling in the blue air.
They could not stop what was written
but kept their watch.
Yes, the blood watered the field
and the grass grew green.
The field, the field at least,
was grateful for this.

Blue Angels

These are thy glorious works, parent of good.
—John Milton, Paradise Lost *Book Five, line 153*

Deep in summer and hot the roar
that traces the river road.
Blue Angels have come from the Air Fair
flying in *delta formation.*

My sons—not quite two, not quite four—
pick up sticks and waggle them at the jets,
testing the air with broken branches.

Under a limitless sky,
Blue Angels arc across the garden.
The Four of Diamonds hector the Opposite Solo
as they roll to *Section High Alpha*
while somewhere north, the Lead Solo,
unseen by us now, swoops low across a runway
doing *the famous sneak pass.*

The garden is filled with blue butterflies,
their wings dotted black and gold—
butterflies that eat only the sweetness of lupine.
Nothing will grow where lupine grows.

After the Fall, after the loss
of Paradise, when God stopped speaking,
the angels sang *Hallelujah,*
in voices as loud as the sea. *Just are thy ways,*
they sang, *righteous are thy decrees*
on all thy works; who can extenuate thee?

And God gave his angels many tasks
to afflict the world, and thus began
outrage from lifeless things.

I know Satan has the better part
in Milton's poem,
but God persists in the face of all cleverness.
God works on and on, revising his mysterious plan.
Who are we, sweating in the garden,
against his mysterious plan?

My children are frightened; they weep
and cannot stop. The Blue Angels turn,
their afterburners light up,
the air is aflutter with indifferent butterflies
and deadly flowers wag their nectared heads.
The garden shudders under the thrust
of those great engines—
Blue Angels rising, disappearing,
my sons waving sticks at the blue sky.

Mason's Kitchenettes

After you, I lived out by the airstrip.
Beyond the Sharp-'n-All and radiator shop,
below the red sign,
with its half-lit, ischemic neon.

Dave and Becky lived next door.

Dave had an Electra Glide
and wanted to go north
for the Blessing of the Bikes.
He asked, Could Becky and I drive behind him
in case he needed his tools?

Montoya was three doors down
and lived on bluegills and Tang.
He kept a Milagro cross,
pounding all his troubles to the wood.

"Watch out for Becky," Dave said,
when he made a run with his "Bros."

So I took her to the putt-putt golf,
where the green witch-head
took the balls putted up her tongue
and spat them from her pointy ears:
right to par, and left, to Bogeyland,
where no one wanted to go.

I sat in the dark with the radio on,
cigarettes scouring the walls.
The dark that through those summer days

was less than half of everything.
Then that first flight—the thrum of turboprops,
answered by the yelp of the manager's dog,
that woke up every morning
as if it'd never lived before.

You say this wasn't a life?
All night, the groan of amphibians
along the weedy ditch.
Becky and I in Bogeyland,
Montoya with a knife in his callused palm,
patiently working a bucket of fish.

The Fish Lamp on the Cover of *Coastal Living* Magazine

As scup or drum, his realm is the open sea,
but now, this living room: the chintz
and brocades, a tidy reef of table and vase.
He's made of rice and chrysanthemums,
the slurry pressed beneath a stone,
then fingered across a bamboo frame.
His fins splay out and paper eyes bulge,
as if his equilibrium—pinioned
atop a metal pole, body puffed full
of sixty watts and air—astonishes.
That lyric, *Too many fish in the sea?*
He croaks and hums and whistles along.
And the dark that sails beyond the window—
he has never seen such dark water.

Glaucoma

The loss is slow to arrive.
A narrowing of the canals
that lead from the eyes
and the edges erode,
the peripheral field dissolves
to a haze of green and gray.
The mailbox is gone,
children in a snowbank, a crow
turning its head in a walnut tree.
A tunneling of sight that comes with age,
layered over near sight, far sight,
haloed lights, the go-slow response of the iris.
The pressure builds within my eyes,
within and then behind; headaches throb
in the afternoons.
The flagstones heave slightly
in the early days of winter,
treacherous when no one is watching.
Until the loss is finally a loss.
I will not walk this way again.

■ ■

The things I'll never see
weigh against what I have:
the moon alone above the pines,
a swirl of river,
water-skin like a snake's skin,
the silence of my daughter
in her armchair by the window,
radio hissing jazz from forty miles distant,
poplars in two feet of snow

and the moon again—
behind the clouds, drifting.

■ ■

Atop a ladder, I chop ice at the eaves,
fearing winter may destroy my house.
The ice is gray and stained by leaves—
umber stains against the yellow siding.
From the fourth rung I look in
to see twelve oranges in a blue ceramic bowl,
fired as the sun breaks
through the scudding clouds.
The oranges are rough and cool to the touch.
a latent sweetness—the sun, the bowl,
the nippled fruit.

■ ■

"Tunnel vision" implies loss at the margins,
a snow-covered hedge and the plow looming behind it.
Or a life with no exits. The way John Donne,
walking through Mitcham in a crisis of faith,
saw only the pismire ahead—
the muck barely crusting,
a way too fetid to freeze.
Does he see clearly, or has he lost the world
beyond the troubles of his own life,
turning and turning?
My daughter, back from seeing the ballet,
explains the Cowgirl's love for the Wrangler
by drawing the Cowgirl's eyes popping from her head,
eyes distorted to the shape of love:
Heart, heart, heart, heart.
Who is the artist who can draw such attention?

■ ■

They choir in the wood lot—
a list of birds judged otherwise useless:
blackbirds, cowbirds, grackles,
iridescent starlings—
swirl like smoke against a darkling sky,
then settle for a time, a rasping,
cacophonous applause
against more powerful weather.
Their song *defies*, it has no melody.
They explode from the pines
and are gone.

■ ■

Following Wilson's original design,
I tried to build a cloud chamber
in an old brass meter,
a way to trace the wake of an electron
across a vapor field. That was years ago;
the first time I failed science.
I wanted to map the passage of light
from molecule to molecule,
to see through the round glass—
sparks, bonded to water and passing on.
Now, reduced to four senses,
I follow my dog through the trees
and stop at the clearing, where,
last summer, I planted a row of sage.
I pull the leaves to my face
and roll them between my fingers,
until my hand is a pungent mix
of pepper, mint, and hay.

■ ■

At the doctor's office,
I am pronounced "glaucoma suspect,"

as in one who committed the crime
with malice aforethought, loved ones bludgeoned
in a cold rage. I am told it can be held,
arrested with drops, artificial tears
that permit the *aqueous humor* to flow
unimpeded. To say it clearly,
to weep is to see the world.
And so this final test:
my chin at rest, tiny meteors of light
whir through a twilight field
around my face. My task—
to tap a bar as the lights appear,
creating the data from which
my vision will be traced.
The lights come at me, faster,
slowing. A picture builds within the machine
of what has been lost
and what can be saved.
And this is where I begin the poem,
undone, stars blowing by and the wings of birds
fluttering at the margins.
O, this round earth, O,
the world's imagined corners.

In Ambient Light

My love is so small.
My love is a bird fluttering near
a cut orange. Or my love is a moth,
coming again to light.

My heart is a one-room cottage.
Have you ever lived in a one-room cottage?
I paid rent by the week
and the stove was a step from my bed.

I was grateful to be held by its walls.

Now I live near a cheap motel.
It's where people have affairs.
Where they blow smoke at the empty pool
and wait out the divorce.
At night I see them come and go
under the sodium vapor lamp.
Sometimes I catch an angry phrase
or a familiar song drifts
from someone's tinny radio.

The light casts shadows across my yard.
We call this ambient light. It's hard
to find stars through its artificial glare,
to see what else is there. The firefly,
for instance, crossing the black ribbon of road.

I find him when he descends—
haloed in the grass. With a tiny heart,

who wouldn't fly from the darkness?
I cup him in my hands
and lift him back into the air.

Obbligato

—*South Hadley, Massachusetts*

This morning I walk to the village,
past the half-built bandstand
on the ragged green. Summer—
an easy time to wander among strangers.
In the coffee shop, the men talk of cures
for aching joints. I walk back,
my body accepting its age,
though last week, my heart panicked again
in the rickety cage of my chest.

Outside my window, the sound of water
falling over a dam; as in, all night,
That's water over the dam, the sparrows
fledged in the trees. My coffee is black,
steam rising. I write, *To love again*
what I once loved, as if to make it so,
lay my watch across the field of my desk.

Last night, at sunset, from somewhere
out across the bronze-colored pond,
a woman sang a single Latin phrase
again and again. I could not find her body
among the mulberry trees
and swamp azaleas, could not quite
discern her words above the falls,
though I once knew this language.
But the task she had set, moving dead words
against a darkening sky! Her voice rising,
night coming on.

Letter to M., from Swannanoa

—Swannanoa, North Carolina

Twilight in the garden, looking across
to where Black Mountain rises.
I'm working through the collection,
the middle poems written, still
unsure how it will end. The days
stay noisy. The drone of mowers,
the college kids baling the first cut of hay,
now and then bucking the fallen
back onto a trailer. What I first took
to be a scarlet tanager's call
was their truck—backing, warning.
In the gathering dark,
the lilies and azaleas reach west.
These, the meadow beauties
and asters, were all worked today
by hummingbirds,
an almost invisible blur of wings,
and I began out of that energy—
cutting an ending that did not end—
though when I passed the garden
at full noon, the dragonflies were making love,
dazzled, head-to-tail.
Tonight, I'm thinking about language
and the silence after. Not the beauty,
but the heft of words,
weighing them in my hands.
At dinner, Gretchen spoke of a reading
given entirely in sign language.
How the poet began,

her hands held above her right shoulder,
the fingered words traveling
through the stanzas,
crossing to the lower left.
At the very crux of each poem,
she worked directly over her heart.
I think of us apart, how you ended
last night's phone call—angry, exhausted.
Knowing you are asleep
will keep me awake tonight,
considering order in the final section,
wanting to call, wake you at dawn
and say, "It's finished,"
the way a stonemason, high on a scaffold,
taps and turns the stones, fitting them, one
by one, into the chimney's rise. At some point,
he climbs down, packs his tools
and goes home.
It must be a simple calculation:
how much weight can the footings hold?

Lilacs for Instance

What is the purpose of green or of blue?
—Rainer Maria Rilke

How I believe a time comes
when they will not bloom again
and later find it isn't true.
Thus, the house down the road—
overgrown with flowering lilacs.
At night I walk a path behind it
coming up along the creek.
Framed in a second-story window,
a woman stands in a green kimono,
toweling herself after a bath.
The silk of her robe falls back
to expose the areola of one breast
and the shadow of her sex, lush
as the flowers that encircle
the house, her bedroom window
lit like a painting from Bonnard.
I pause in the looming dark,
tongue thick with the fragrance
of lilacs, until she turns out
her light. After which there are
always lilacs, and the sweet music
of a distant song.

Biopsy

They call it *fine needle*,
not for any beauty
in the sharp itself, but because
it is *thin, keen, attenuated*—
a point brought so delicately to your throat,
you said you felt only
motion: pressure against the skin,
then a slight wiggle of the doctor's hand
and the needle withdrawn.
The nurse brought me to you
and we drove home in near silence,
the bandage on your neck
marked by a dot of blood.
After you were settled
with your magazines, a cup of tea,
your chestnut hair lit by the sunlight
of that October afternoon,
I went back to work—having no choice,
I claimed—and as I drove
south of town, I saw wrens
massed in a stand of trees, fluttering
down—two, four, three-after-one—
because that is the way of wrens, gathered
in autumn. They were lit
by the same light as your hair, the trees—
they were aspens—gold, and the birds' wings
illumined, front and back. Then,
in my blind spot, I lost the wrens
and became almost frantic, until *Yes,* they came
again in the rearview mirror—their wings
lit up, their bodies still fluttering
endlessly to ground.

After the Diagnosis

These cells have destroyed large portions of the gland.
The presence of capsular and vascular invasion suggests
the prognosis may not be as favorable as usually seen.
                                               —*Pathology report*

At 3 AM, I leave the house
and follow the footsteps of the cat
through a dusting of snow.
I lose her trail near the white pines,
the moon—resected and luminous,
somewhere out across the lake.
I want to walk through the trees
and along the creek
to where the path breaks through
to open water. Though I won't go
so far. This wind is coarse
and I'm not dressed against the cold;
the stars, at best, are far-off fires.
They caress nothing. You are
so tired since coming home—
a second smile
newly stitched across your throat.
Between the moment when
the great horned owl
ceases to mourn for the vole
and the last train before dawn,
the cold rebuilds its silence
in the trees. No elegies.
This winter is just one more darkness
we must learn to walk through.

Swimming at Night

I go back to the river,
crossing the tangle of buckthorn
and trailing bittersweet.

Moonlight and the scrotal cold,
the mayflies, unmoored, drift with me.

I remember making love at the river's edge
and after, how she sang a small song,
the last I heard her sing.

Wire embedded in trees,
rusted where a fence line failed.
The heron stalks the shallows.
Not even my body frightens her away.

Where are you bound, mayflies
adrift, elegant moon-deaf bird?
My dead will not come home.

If water asks that I go to the sea
I must go with it.

Elegy for Light and Balance

*In his seascapes, [Winslow] Homer depended on narrative structures
that would, just as they began to suggest a normal unfolding, deflect
the viewer from obvious and easy interpretations.*

—*Notes from a catalog*

Driving the winter road
that falls through the blueberry field.
Rows flicker as I pass, red letters
igniting a page of snow,
with my house, that gray paragraph
on the left. The road is aswirl, snow
so thick I might fall under its spell,
and will—my inner ear's infected.
I step into the drive,
let go the car door, the cinders blurred
with ice. And then—
the howl of wind, a too-slick sole,
my body saying, *I am not cured.*

■ ■

In the old cartoons, when a clown
is struck with a mallet, the birds twitter
around his head, rising and falling,
the way the swallows rose
that summer evening, you and I
in the gathering dark. They were so close—
their wings arced, then beat into a vast open.
We walked out into the field,
the moon alive and everything luminous—your face,
my hands—one dancer balancing another.
That night, your body pulling mine,

the simple hunger—your small
bird-like shudder, a swallow fluttering to leave
the lip of her nest.

■ ■

To the unconscious mind,
any leap is possible—
the drunk stumbling along a cliff,
or the soul, harp in hand, lifting away
from the fallen clown—the music sweet, so sweet
we catch our breath and turn
when the soul-clown strums and wavers,
deciding whether to go on.

■ ■

The snow begins again—
what the painter would not paint
until his last years in Maine—
snow swirling and a man along a cliff,
the howl of wind through dead sea grasses,
all his options in the air. The seasons whirl
and turn on themselves, the planets slow
but spin back,
so many china plates set awhirl on wobbly sticks
in a show I saw as a child,
never falling until the juggler,
glittering in his beaded tights, said,
They must. I could hardly catch my breath
for the motion and the shine of it. Last week,
ear howling, reeling as I haven't reeled
in ten sober years,
I circled the shed I meant for a studio,
my books inside and tables I might work at.
The glass caught fire in the day's last light,

snow adrift against the door,
wanting someone to open it.

■ ■

Coming to, my lungs chuff to open,
waves pulling the empty suck,
gasping and then gasping again.
In my good ear, it could be crows,
who dance in the field
and do not trust the sea—
my lip numb and a taste of blood,
the sea salt and metal, where my face struck the ice.
What story could I have told, rising on one elbow,
casually looking out into the red-lettered world,
even as the world slowly turned to white?

■ ■

I kept the catalog you gave me
from the museum in Boston.
It says that in the dead of winter,
Homer began *A Summer Night:*
two girls dancing along a cliff,
their hands so delicately assembled
and bodies circling—
a song one can almost hear and the sea,
breaking, out among the kelp and limpets.
The moon isn't shown, though its light
is fully arrayed,
and the bodies of those who watch—do they watch
the dancers or the sea?—are silhouettes along the edge.
The sky is deep indigo, but here and there, and then
in great swatches, moonlight renders the waves
a cerulean blue; it fairy-swirls across the page.
And the dancers glow, back-lit,
in perfect balance with the waves.

For months, he reworked the canvas,
finally adding the floor they dance on.
It is an odd detail.
Does he mean to keep the dancers safe,
though moonlight lifts the waves
and the bodies along the cliff
lean back, vertiginous, forever falling
toward the sea?

III

The Body, Burning

Flame is a red-hot vapor, fume, or exhalation—
For flaming bodies emit fumes that burn in the flame.
                    —Sir Isaac Newton
                    Opticks, Book III, Part 1

Let us speak of cases.
The woman who spontaneously ignites

at the Fenwick Apartments,
air filled with smoke, walls thick

with soot, radio playing static
across the angles

of the courtyard. Or those lovers
running from a London flat,

arms raised and bodies aflame,
bits of scorched cloth

fluttering in their wake.

Among the exotica,
the police found no accelerant.

And what of the carnival man,
an "intemperate drinker of drams,"

smoldering in a filthy bed,

"Dead," the priest decrees,
"by visitation of God"?

For Newton, fire *is* the body.
For Bonaventure it's the soul,

burning on its journey into God.
A line is crossed

and when the moment comes
who can stand against it?

The body gradually lessened,
dreamed into grace,

laying out
what is needed for another life.

What does the body want?
To be a crucible, says the body.

The seraphim,

these six-winged angels
fanning the body to flames,

the rapture. This passage
into Jerusalem.

Hay Devil

Flat the field. The hay cut
and dry under an afternoon sun.
It is a black car speeding along the road
that first churns the air.
Soon, what is here cannot
resist, and I stand as the hay rises—
twenty, forty, sixty feet—
raveling into the vacuous blue
then toppling, toppling.
From across the field
I come to the whirlwind
and step into the lifting straw,
as if I might ascend
the fabled ladder of heaven.
And *Behold,* my body
disrupts the roaring throat
and the vortex
hesitates and then re-forms.
What wind-blind fool, deafened,
staggers from his knees
and enters the spiraling chimney
again? Yes, this is my body.
Oh yes, I am your fool.

Discontinuous Narrative

My vasectomy, for instance.
I choose a woman doctor,
admiring William the Conqueror
and his great French broadsword,
but frankly, preferring the glories
of the Bayeux Tapestry;
the art of the women's stitch work—
the terra cotta and blue-green threads,
the olives and the goldenrod.
It has endured nearly a thousand years,
cut to pieces during wartime or plague
and years later, reassembled,
like a silent film, rescued at last
from the cutting room floor.
We can't blame them
because the narrative is scrambled,
making another disputed text,
like those misplaced scenes
where the bird-flingers hurl pigeons
at the fearsome hawks,
or the nameless oafs are either
floundering in the surf or diving for eels.
Sacre bleu! She cuts so well—
the *vas deferentia* pulled through,
right then left, the buzz
of the cauterization—like a honeybee
working a *fleur-de-lis.*
Yes, my vasectomy, my midlife stumble
through the blazed tail of a fateful star
seems to you a child's sparkler
given a desultory wave on a hot summer night,

while I see it marshalling the tragic rhythms
of Norse heroic poetry—
Never again my longship setting sail
with lanterns fixed to its masthead,
never again the brigands wielding
their great swords and beflagged lances.
Oh, here is *The Patient's Tale*—
the leaky wineskin of my scrotum,
a weekend aboard the couch,
the lost-kingdom feeling
that lingers for days.
As in the tapestry's last panel—
how a single horse with one terrified rider,
pursued by Norman dogs, kicks
and plunges forever onward:
into the undyed backing,
across the frayed and unmapped fens.

Letter to the Chairwoman of the Reunion Committee

It is enough if I manage
to be a poet among the savages.
      —Ovid, Letter to Rome from exile among the Getae.
            Letters From Pontus, *Book I,* 5.65

I knew you as cheerleader—
hands clapping, the cold smoke of your breath,
the year the Centurions went 10-and-0,
your eyes enslaving my heart,
high in the student section.
In World Lit, in Latin,
or the night you took the throne
as Homecoming Queen,
the night Mike Hurd loped sixty yards
to thrash the Gaels. Now your letter arrives,
calling me home.

The truth is, I've lost our yearbook,
and must add thirty years to a memory
to find you in a suburban study,
reading my response. Julie,
I was married and divorced
and left a woman not unlike yourself
with a bitter heart.
I am married again, to a painter of nudes
and human forms,
who found me speaking tongues
among the wallet makers.
Her palette is deep green and cobalt,
rose madder and the colors of the body.

I've lost touch with everyone—Randy and Tom,
Mike, Laura, and Diane. I know that beautiful Lynn,
whom I loved, is dead,
that two boys I didn't know well
were killed in the war. I milled at the barricades,
threw a rock from a cloud of tear gas,
a single palm-sized rock.
I can't say where it landed.
But Julie, the dead were finally dead.
It came to nothing.
Now my dog waits at the door, regards me
with that mix of need and pathos
that is the way of Labradors.
So we walk into another starred night,
spring again but too far north, the trees not knowing
what to say, though if years tell us anything,
leaves will come.
I could say Orion watches the Dragon,
who stares at the fussy cloud of the Crow,
that the moon is a silver hanger—
what our parents called
The old moon in the new moon's arms,
though it probably isn't true.
I can't remember the stars, vague shapes
confuse me now, don't know what to call the moon.
Regardless, my dog arcs his leg,
steam rising from the mighty work
of marking his range.
Hard to believe this sweet dog relates
so closely to wolves, differing only
in his desire for comfort,
by the passage of time.

Do you remember Mr. Murphy,
who made us read *The Brothers Karamazov?*

That good man, dripping with sweat on the coldest days,
shaky hand ascending to his forehead,
when asked to explain what Dmitri says
at page 163: "What seems disgraceful to the mind,
is beauty, and nothing else, to the heart."
What to make, then, of the party at Danny Hansen's,
when Diane went off with the boy from Jackson High?
You found me in the dark, a car-length
from his yellow Firebird, watching
as they made love, bodies thrown so recklessly
across the bucket seats, that with each thrust
Diane's head banged a half-opened door free,
igniting the dome light, again and
again. I did not look away.
When I saw you watching me,
I looked at you with embarrassment
and desire. What could you have known?
How could you run for the porch,
leaving me, for thirty years, unable
to explain, to make a better response than
"It's not what you think,"
though it surely was? Under siege,
beset by ramping device,
the heart tries to account for itself.
And in truth, I have watched the troika go over the cliff
with more than passing interest.

No, I won't be there in October.
I can't ride atop the Class Float,
like those Roman generals
Mr. Smith droned on about in Latin III.
But I ran the mile, remember?
and longer, further, in cross country.
No speed even then, but I could go a distance.
Perhaps I could jog along beside you

like a conquered slave, dragged back from war
along the Danube, arrayed in my animal skins,
uncouth, but chastened by events,
too stunned to speak of my simple life,
my true life—among the wolves,
among the Getae.

Dancing with the Crack Whores, at the Homeless Shelter Run by My Wife

Wendy is leaving the shelter.
With six months clean,
it's time to let her go.
Someone slides "Love and Happiness"
into Angel's boom box.
We are hard by the Projects,
ten blocks of two-story drug deals
and boarded up windows, graffitied
in street-gang cursive,
the great failed experiment
of this unlettered, pig-iron city.
The women want to teach us "the Hustle,"
a line dance from years ago,
though the steps have gotten more complex.
Something that can make you do wrong
Or make you do right, Al Green whispers,
Lo-ove and happiness.
The bass line rumbles, a half shang-a-lang
of guitar, and the women move—
three steps right, back, a side-step,
three left. They clap once and repeat, until
everyone has it down.
Love is, Al sings, *walking together—*
his voice rising now, like a pressure valve
at work over some great fire—*talking together.*
The Memphis Horns ascend eight notes,
repeat the last two—
Make you wanna dance,
Love and happiness.
I can't handle the half-turn and step away,

wanting to know how this song would play
without the Hammond B-3
loping the melody,
but Angel laughs and pulls at my arm,
rolls her thigh in a stop-action
turn, and is back with the others,
perfectly on beat. Al sings,
We'll see each other,
Walk away with victo-ry.
My wife follows Wendy down the line,
as if their bodies are passing along a wire.
Love is, Al groans, *Love is,*
and for a moment, Yes,
love is rapturous,
but what must we do to be saved?
We are dancing Wendy into the world,
where she will last a month.
Next week, Angel will pick a fight at lunch,
leave in a chorus of sobs
and be dead within the year.
Don't ask about her baby.
In the Projects, to stand with your arms in the air
means, *I am ready to buy or sell.*
I see the women, when the cars roll by,
opening like tulips.

Were We Speaking, Had You Asked

I'd bring you cauliflower
and the leaf tips of artichokes.
Or tiny radishes and
wild fennel, the violet ribs
of chard, shorn of all flesh;
sliced gingerroot, the woody hearts
of parsnips—acidic, astringent.
You might try the leeks:
one end spring green, the other—
forged in mud—
resplendent, bone white.
You might cut through the pulp
of these purple beets,
splay them across wilted
spinach, swirl them
with turnips, pungent mustard
greens, weedy amaranth
or rapini, slightly past its prime,
sauté them all with olive oil
and chopped garlic.
Are they bitter?
That is something best known
at the root of the tongue, where
muscle and blood run thick,
where the nerve ends *fire,*
fire, fire at whatever starts to gag,
snapping shut the voice box
and binding the heart to silence.

Letter to Robert in Gearhart

—Gearhart, Oregon

Hard not to think of you
as an ancient sea-dwelling god—
gray beard, rake in hand, full gale
at your back, lifting strands of holiday lights
into a fierce Pacific rain.
A rough go this year: Tre's death,
inexplicable and too early, leaving
only her work—the burnished clay,
her tragic figurines—
your children and grandchildren
scattered among the various states.
Still, you go on. A prelude at the piano,
the flicker of the nightly news,
one glass of red wine.
Sanderlings scramble along the beach, right
then left. Sleet changes to rain, then back
again, the wind roaring in
from across half a world—ceaseless,
like some vast oceanic wheel
that turns and grinds at the heart.

Descent

It was the summer of moths,
the lake aswarm with wings—
bodies thrown where the waves broke
and those that survived
rose and fell among the phlox.
You were awaiting the child
we had not expected,
rolling through the ocean of your womb.
It was time for the skull to engage the pelvis,
a lightening that would tell us
the descent had begun.
Child, what will I do with you?
I was reading Milton, lost
in the early books. Knowing the blind poet
spoke each line to his daughters—
the years it took to say and write them down.
And the moths came,
wet and ragged from flight.
I picked one up and rubbed its wings
till my fingers shone in the near dark.
They might have been living things
or stars burning low, beyond pine trees
and ash.

Carolina Woodpecker

He works the loblolly pines
outside the screened porch,
where a lightning strike sheared three trees
to yellow bone. In another life,
I'd say he was a writer, working
through a block. The lines come hard,
each phrase parsed out. But this one
persists—his vermilion head
hammering out larvae and bark beetles.
The day dissolves like a sugar cube.
I lean against the door frame
with a cup of coffee, admiring
what he knows about the margins,
his hunger that pounds on and on.

At 48, Walking My Baby Past the Voodoo Lounge

"A few children for me of my own, is that excessive? No, . . . It is the right moment, just right."
                    -Edgar Degas, letter from New Orleans to Henri Rouart

I wheel his stroller across Bienville,
turn left on Chartres, pause at the house
where Napoleon planned to brood
his final years. Carlos doesn't care—
napping under a blanket I've spread
to keep him from the sun. The sidewalks
are sticky, the air—roiling with booze
and boiled shrimp, and the music won't stop—
at every door, the chank-a-chank of zydeco,
or drum machines rat-tatting
into the street. I light a cigar.
We are men-about-town, me pointing out
the gaslights and balconies, the walls
brushed aquamarine, chiffon, or a sweet
sun-ripened pink. On Toulouse,
he spots two beagles, who, scampering round
their tiny yard, make him laugh, as they tumble
against an iron fence. I prop Carlos at the gate
and snap a picture, in which he looks
straight at the camera, smiling slyly,
like the smallest child in Degas's painting
Children on a Doorstep—the light,
that same goldenrod—with a beagle
posed at a distance. You say
it's crazy to have this new child.
You think even worse.

I only know that under the sign
"Famous Live Love Acts of New Orleans,"
I look at Carlos and smile.
And passing the Voodoo Lounge, I know
that no bad luck can touch us now.

Blackbirds

Who wrote these lyrics?
Glottal, the sound of water, worried
over jagged rocks. Then louder—
blackbirds flocked in the pines.
The dogs twirl and snap the air, the birds,
a near riot, rise.
Our year-old son, wide-eyed
against my shoulder, begins to wave,
his fingers like little tongues
mouthing, *No one here can love
or understand me,* his song lost
in the protest of the flock.
The first to break are already
a quarter-mile gone. Birdbrains,
they have forgotten our trees—
the amber sap and green needles—
though the flock tails back to us,
shape-shifting, a ragged scarf
beating across the blueberry flats
and over-flying the river,
where rusty freighters unload salt
all night at the docks. Here,
blackbirds still rattle the pines,
while across the yard,
hundreds more croak the chorus,
until the stragglers lift
and we are shouting at silence,
our son's hand still working
his hard-luck story at the sky.

The Salt Cairn

—Seaside, Oregon

Winter at the end of the trail,
where the Columbia washes the ocean,
what one book calls *The Kingdom of Conifers*
and you, "the prettiest greens":
cedars, hemlock, Douglas fir.
Here, Clark sent his salt makers
across the scuffled dunes, to make a salt
that was *excellent, strong & white.*
We are coughing, our lungs thick
with a cold we carried
through the taffy shop and pinball palace
to a carousel that no one rides
in this ragged carnival town.
Did the salt makers camp near the end of this block?
I search for the cairn. To my left,
an anvil of headland stretches away,
beyond me, the ocean heaves forever shoreward.
The air is salt and wood smoke, the rain,
good in my lungs. Twenty minutes go by
before I find it—
cemented together by the village Lions
and squared in a wrought iron fence,
five kettles atop the fitted stones.
I have dragged you into a salt maker's life.
What will become of us?
You singing to the sleeping child,
me boiling the ocean down
to whatever is good, to what remains.

Lepidopterist

Daggerwing, Longwing, Metalmark.
How would it feel to be the boy again
who knew the names of butterflies?
Field guide in hand, a silver canteen,
hiding among the melons
in my father's ragged garden,
among the fronds of asparagus gone to seed.
Now, I see the simplest things—
how Sulphurs come to cigar smoke,
that Swallowtails flutter
among the milkweeds, a Monarch
at rest upon the woodpile.
It's why I leave the spider web
hanging in the doorway, I think,
weighed down by the husk
of a caterpillar. Letting the web hang
into November. Beyond.

On a Visit to His Namesake City, St. Paul Walks Six Blocks of Goodrich Avenue

He turns at the Lutheran Church
and walks the first block. It is good
in the gathering dusk—the stuccoed homes,
sprinklers ratcheting the lawns.
He sidesteps a tricycle, stops
to smell the lilies and the heliotropes.
From the windows of a bungalow,
the sound of Spyro Gyra lofts into the street,
trumpet and sax swirling through the smoke
of burgers on the grill.
He hikes his robes, does a little dance, then
cautions himself, though he knows that a dance,
an act of simple joy, isn't always
an occasion for sin. A woman crosses
Pascal Street, towing a child in a red wagon.
Paul thinks, *Yes,* I could walk with them,
patiently pull that wagon, kindly
wipe the child's nose, perhaps
talk on the ways of hummingbirds.
He considers taking a wife.
Thinks twice. *Better though, to marry*
than to burn. On this street—
among the eighty-year-old homes,
the flower pots and Subarus,
he can't imagine honky-tonks
or country music. But service clubs
and string quartets, an ice cream social,
the sonorous voice of Garrison Keillor
each Saturday at five—
even with that small penance—

it would be a good life. It comforts him
to think of it: four bedrooms and a chopping block,
a spa on the modest deck,
a wife to call when he was on the road,
preaching in the shopping malls.
He does not dwell upon the wolf of winter.
Where the pavement ends at a precipice,
he turns back. He remembers
the burgers on that grill—thinks,
on a street like this, a tired man,
a man who has walked for many years
pursuing the Lord's work, surely he could step
into a neighbor's yard and say *Hello!*
Begin with talk of the various fescues,
or how the nasturtiums are coming in,
nurse a glass of wine for his stomach's sake
and talk on until dark about the Twins.